Hugo and Flo to the Rescue

By Cameron Macintosh

Hugo lives in Europe.
But he grew up on
the Sunshine Coast.

Hugo's mum cleans paintings to make them look like new.

Hugo's school is a music school.

Hugo must make up a song. But he does not have a clue what type of song to make!

Hugo calls his pal Flo for help.

Flo lives a long way away.
She has a funny little rescue dog.

Help, Flo!
What type of song should
I make for music school?

I will think on it, Hugo!
Thanks! What did you do at school today?

“We have been studying painting for a few weeks,” said Flo. “I have to paint something!”

What should I paint?
It's due on Tuesday!

My mum is cleaning
that painting.
It's called a "still life".
I can paint a still life
in bright hues!
I will use blue and pink!

I can help with your music, Hugo!

Flo sent Hugo a few music files.

Hugo clicked the menu and then on a file.

Jazz music played!

CHECKING FOR MEANING

1. What does Hugo's mum do with the paintings she works on? *(Literal)*
2. Where does Hugo live? *(Literal)*
3. How did Hugo and Flo "rescue" each other? *(Inferential)*

EXTENDING VOCABULARY

Europe	Where is Europe? Can you name some countries in Europe?
rescue	What does it mean to rescue something? What is another word the author could have used instead of *rescue*? What does it mean that Flo's dog is a rescue dog?
hues	What does the word *hues* mean? What is another word with a similar meaning? What is your favourite hue or colour?

MOVING BEYOND THE TEXT

1. Flo and Hugo needed help with ideas for their projects. Why is it a good idea to ask for help? Have you ever needed help?

2. How might someone clean an old painting to look like new? What tools might they need? What might be difficult about cleaning a painting?

3. Hugo and Flo live in different parts of the world. They stay friends by video-calling each other. What are some other ways we can stay in touch with friends and family who don't live close to us?

4. Flo's dad plays the drums, and Hugo plays the ukulele. Do you play or would you like to play a musical instrument? What instrument?

TIME TO WRITE

Think about what happened next in this story. Pretend you are Flo or Hugo, and write about how your project turned out.

PRACTICE WORDS